TABLE OF
CONTENTS

LETTER FROM
PASTOR DALE

What an incredible year 2023 has been so far! God is doing amazing things through our faith family, and He's just getting started. There is so much more to look forward to! We are making an eternal impact today and paying it forward for future generations.

I'm excited to present you with the second volume of **52 Weeks of Forward**, and I hope you enjoyed the first volume as much as I did. Thanks to our staff and leadership, who prayerfully crafted these weekly devotionals for us to read and share as God prompts. We pray that you will be equipped and encouraged in your faith journey.

Every **Moving Forward** section provides a practical step to begin living out each timely lesson. We've also created a space to journal your thoughts and prayers. God has so much in store for us. We are His light to a world in desperate need of Him.

When we immerse ourselves in Scripture, it impacts every area of our lives. That's why we've included a daily Bible reading plan that follows the order in which historical events unfolded. You can join us in reading the Bible in a year or take it at a different pace. God's Word will surely bring healing and fresh wisdom to your life. Volume one included the reading plan for January through June; volume two begins in July and will guide us through the end of December.

May the Bible reading plan and devotionals equip you to participate in God's redemptive story and share it with others. Let's continue to **Move Forward** with faith. God has so much more for us in the remainder of 2023 and beyond!

Dale Oquist
LEAD PASTOR

READ THE
BIBLE IN A YEAR

We are transformed by reading God's Word because it is living and active! Enjoy the second half of the comprehensive reading plan below. You can join us in reading through the Bible in a year or complete it at your own pace. It continues to take us through the chronology of events unfolding throughout history. Let's **Move Forward** together!

WEEK 1: JUL 2 - 8

- [ ] **SUN**   2 Kings 1-4
- [ ] **MON**   2 Kings 5-8
- [ ] **TUE**   2 Kings 9-11
- [ ] **WED**   2 Kings 12-13; 2 Chronicles 24
- [ ] **THU**   2 Kings 14; 2 Chronicles 25
- [ ] **FRI**   Jonah
- [ ] **SAT**   2 Kings 15; 2 Chronicles 26

WEEK 2: JUL 9 - 15

- [ ] **SUN**   Isaiah 1-4
- [ ] **MON**   Isaiah 5-8
- [ ] **TUE**   Amos 1-5
- [ ] **WED**   Amos 6-9
- [ ] **THU**   2 Chronicles 27; Isaiah 9-12
- [ ] **FRI**   Micah
- [ ] **SAT**   2 Chronicles 28; 2 Kings 16-17

WEEK 3: JUL 16 - 22

- [ ] **SUN**   Isaiah 13-17
- [ ] **MON**   Isaiah 18-22
- [ ] **TUE**   Isaiah 23-27
- [ ] **WED**   2 Kings 18; 2 Chronicles 29-31; Psalm 48
- [ ] **THU**   Hosea 1-7
- [ ] **FRI**   Hosea 8-14
- [ ] **SAT**   Isaiah 28-30

WEEK 4: JUL 23 - 29

- [ ] **SUN**   Isaiah 31-34
- [ ] **MON**   Isaiah 35-36
- [ ] **TUE**   Isaiah 37-39; Psalm 76
- [ ] **WED**   Isaiah 40-43
- [ ] **THU**   Isaiah 44-48
- [ ] **FRI**   2 Kings 19; Psalms 46, 80, 135
- [ ] **SAT**   Isaiah 49-53

WEEK 5: JUL 30 - AUG 5

- [ ] **SUN**   Isaiah 54-58
- [ ] **MON**   Isaiah 59-63
- [ ] **TUE**   Isaiah 64-66
- [ ] **WED**   2 Kings 20-21
- [ ] **THU**   2 Chronicles 32-33
- [ ] **FRI**   Nahum
- [ ] **SAT**   2 Kings 22-23; 2 Chronicles 34-35

WEEK 6: AUG 6 - 12

- [ ] **SUN**   Zephaniah
- [ ] **MON**   Jeremiah 1-3
- [ ] **TUE**   Jeremiah 4-6
- [ ] **WED**   Jeremiah 7-9
- [ ] **THU**   Jeremiah 10-13
- [ ] **FRI**   Jeremiah 14-17
- [ ] **SAT**   Jeremiah 18-22

WEEK 7: AUG 13 - 19

- [ ] **SUN**   Jeremiah 23-25
- [ ] **MON**   Jeremiah 26-29
- [ ] **TUE**   Jeremiah 30-31
- [ ] **WED**   Jeremiah 32-34
- [ ] **THU**   Jeremiah 35-37
- [ ] **FRI**   Jeremiah 38-40; Psalms 74, 79
- [ ] **SAT**   2 Kings 24-25; 2 Chronicles 36

WEEK 8: AUG 20 - 26

- [ ] **SUN**   Habakkuk
- [ ] **MON**   Jeremiah 41-45
- [ ] **TUE**   Jeremiah 46-48
- [ ] **WED**   Jeremiah 49-50
- [ ] **THU**   Jeremiah 51-52
- [ ] **FRI**   Lamentations 1-2
- [ ] **SAT**   Lamentations 3-5

WEEK 9: AUG 27 - SEP 2

- [ ] **SUN**   Ezekiel 1-4
- [ ] **MON**   Ezekiel 5-8
- [ ] **TUE**   Ezekiel 9-12
- [ ] **WED**   Ezekiel 13-15
- [ ] **THU**   Ezekiel 16-17
- [ ] **FRI**   Ezekiel 18-20
- [ ] **SAT**   Ezekiel 21-22

WEEK 10: SEP 3 - 9

- [ ] **SUN**   Ezekiel 23-24
- [ ] **MON**   Ezekiel 25-27
- [ ] **TUE**   Ezekiel 28-30
- [ ] **WED**   Ezekiel 31-33
- [ ] **THU**   Ezekiel 34-36
- [ ] **FRI**   Ezekiel 37-39
- [ ] **SAT**   Ezekiel 40-42

WEEK 11: SEP 10 - 16

- [ ] **SUN**   Ezekiel 43-45
- [ ] **MON**   Ezekiel 46-48
- [ ] **TUE**   Joel
- [ ] **WED**   Daniel 1-3
- [ ] **THU**   Daniel 4-6
- [ ] **FRI**   Daniel 7-9
- [ ] **SAT**   Daniel 10-12

WEEK 12: SEP 17 - 23

- [ ] **SUN**   Ezra 1-3
- [ ] **MON**   Ezra 4-6; Psalm 137
- [ ] **TUE**   Haggai
- [ ] **WED**   Zechariah 1-4
- [ ] **THU**   Zechariah 5-9
- [ ] **FRI**   Zechariah 10-14
- [ ] **SAT**   Esther 1-5

→   →   →   →   →   →   →   →   →

→   →   →   →   →   →   →   →   →

→   →   →   →   →   →   →   →   →

WEEK 13: SEP 24 - 30

- [ ] **SUN**   Esther 6-10
- [ ] **MON**   Ezra 7-10
- [ ] **TUE**   Nehemiah 1-5
- [ ] **WED**   Nehemiah 6-7
- [ ] **THU**   Nehemiah 8-10
- [ ] **FRI**   Nehemiah 11-13; Psalm 126
- [ ] **SAT**   Malachi

WEEK 14: OCT 1 - 7

- [ ] **SUN**   Luke 1; John 1
- [ ] **MON**   Matthew 1; Luke 2
- [ ] **TUE**   Matthew 2
- [ ] **WED**   Matthew 3; Mark 1; Luke 3
- [ ] **THU**   Matthew 4; Luke 4-5
- [ ] **FRI**   John 2-4
- [ ] **SAT**   Matthew 8; Mark 2

WEEK 15: OCT 8 - 14

- [ ] **SUN**   John 5
- [ ] **MON**   Matthew 12; Mark 3; Luke 6
- [ ] **TUE**   Matthew 5-7
- [ ] **WED**   Matthew 9; Luke 7
- [ ] **THU**   Matthew 11
- [ ] **FRI**   Luke 11
- [ ] **SAT**   Matthew 13; Luke 8

WEEK 16: OCT 15 - 21

- [ ] **SUN**   Mark 4-5
- [ ] **MON**   Matthew 10
- [ ] **TUE**   Matthew 14; Mark 6; Luke 9
- [ ] **WED**   John 6
- [ ] **THU**   Matthew 15; Mark 7
- [ ] **FRI**   Matthew 16; Mark 8
- [ ] **SAT**   Matthew 17; Mark 9

WEEK 17: OCT 22 - 28

- [ ] **SUN**   Matthew 18
- [ ] **MON**   John 7-8
- [ ] **TUE**   John 9-10
- [ ] **WED**   Luke 10
- [ ] **THU**   Luke 12-13
- [ ] **FRI**   Luke 14-15
- [ ] **SAT**   Luke 16-17

WEEK 18: OCT 29 - NOV 4

- [ ] **SUN**   John 11
- [ ] **MON**   Luke 18
- [ ] **TUE**   Matthew 19; Mark 10
- [ ] **WED**   Matthew 20-21
- [ ] **THU**   Luke 19
- [ ] **FRI**   Mark 11; John 12
- [ ] **SAT**   Matthew 22; Mark 12

WEEK 19: NOV 5 - 11

- [ ] **SUN**   Matthew 23; Luke 20-21
- [ ] **MON**   Mark 13
- [ ] **TUE**   Matthew 24
- [ ] **WED**   Matthew 25
- [ ] **THU**   Matthew 26; Mark 14
- [ ] **FRI**   Luke 22; John 13
- [ ] **SAT**   John 14-17

WEEK 20: NOV 12 - 18

- [ ] **SUN**   Matthew 27; Mark 15
- [ ] **MON**   Luke 23; John 18-19
- [ ] **TUE**   Matthew 28; Mark 16
- [ ] **WED**   Luke 24; John 20-21
- [ ] **THU**   Acts 1-3
- [ ] **FRI**   Acts 4-6
- [ ] **SAT**   Acts 7-8

WEEK 21: NOV 19 - 25

- [ ] **SUN** Acts 9-10
- [ ] **MON** Acts 11-12
- [ ] **TUE** Acts 13-14
- [ ] **WED** James
- [ ] **THU** Acts 15-16
- [ ] **FRI** Galatians 1-3
- [ ] **SAT** Galatians 4-6

WEEK 22: NOV 26 - DEC 2

- [ ] **SUN** Acts 17
- [ ] **MON** 1 & 2 Thessalonians
- [ ] **TUE** Acts 18-19
- [ ] **WED** 1 Corinthians 1-4
- [ ] **THU** 1 Corinthians 5-8
- [ ] **FRI** 1 Corinthians 9-11
- [ ] **SAT** 1 Corinthians 12-14

WEEK 23: DEC 3 - 9

- [ ] **SUN** 1 Corinthians 15-16
- [ ] **MON** 2 Corinthians 1-4
- [ ] **TUE** 2 Corinthians 5-9
- [ ] **WED** 2 Corinthians 10-13
- [ ] **THU** Romans 1-3
- [ ] **FRI** Romans 4-7
- [ ] **SAT** Romans 8-10

WEEK 24: DEC 10 - 16

- [ ] **SUN** Romans 11-13
- [ ] **MON** Romans 14-16
- [ ] **TUE** Acts 20-23
- [ ] **WED** Acts 24-26
- [ ] **THU** Acts 27-28
- [ ] **FRI** Colossians; Philemon
- [ ] **SAT** Ephesians

WEEK 25: DEC 17 - 23

- [ ] **SUN** Philippians; 1 Timothy
- [ ] **MON** Titus
- [ ] **TUE** 1 Peter
- [ ] **WED** Hebrews 1-6
- [ ] **THU** Hebrews 7-10
- [ ] **FRI** Hebrews 11-13
- [ ] **SAT** 2 Timothy

WEEK 26: DEC 24 - 30

- [ ] **SUN** 2 Peter; Jude
- [ ] **MON** 1 John
- [ ] **TUE** 2 & 3 John
- [ ] **WED** Revelation 1-5
- [ ] **THU** Revelation 6-11
- [ ] **FRI** Revelation 12-18
- [ ] **SAT** Revelation 19-22

→ → → → → → → → → → → → → → → → → →
→ → → → → → → → → → → → → → → → → →
→ → → → → → → → → → → → → → → → → →
→ → → → → → → → → → → → → → → → → →
→ → → → → → → → → → → → → → → → → →

FUTURE PSALMS

BY PASTOR DALE OQUIST

**SING TO THE LORD; PRAISE HIS NAME.
EACH DAY PROCLAIM THE GOOD NEWS THAT HE SAVES.**

PSALM 96:2 (NLT)

The Psalms are fascinatingly complex. When we think of the Psalms, we think of uplifting, encouraging, and sweeping passages that praise God's goodness, faithfulness, and mercy. We think of Psalm 23 and its beautiful imagery. We think of the protection and provision in Psalm 91 or the thankfulness in Psalm 138.

But there are also Psalms of lament (Psalm 13), exhaustion (Psalm 6), shame (Psalm 131), hurt (Psalm 55), guilt (Psalm 130), injustice (Psalm 7), and feeling abandoned by God (Psalm 22). The Psalms have been used to help people with post-traumatic stress disorder and those experiencing loss and anger through debilitating circumstances.

This book is unique, and its origin is the reason it is so captivating. God inspires every book of the Bible; however, the Psalms are special because they are not words from a human writer to a human audience. They are a collection of songs, poems, and ideas from human writers to God. It is the most extensive collection of words to God in the Bible.

We have found solace and camaraderie with people who wrote these Psalms thousands of years ago. We think, "If they could withstand their struggles, I can withstand mine!" Their human experience speaks to us and helps us understand our trials and difficulties. Their anguish helps with our grief. Their praise in turbulent circumstances helps us weather and praise Him through the storm.

But these are not the only psalms that future generations should read. There are psalms inside of you that only you can write. Led by the Holy Spirit, your words could encourage future generations you'll never meet, emboldening them by your faith as they connect with your shared experience.

Your family (and beyond) should read about your experiences and how God faithfully led you through prosperous times and times of want. They should bear witness to how you express your adoration toward God when everything else is falling around you. The psalms you write will not be added to the canon of Scripture but could be added to your family's legacy. Your influence will stretch far beyond your years, and future generations will find comfort in your words and solidarity during life's storms simply because you wrote down your psalms of praise to God.

 ## MOVING FORWARD

Write your psalm. How has God led you through painful challenges? What dilemmas are you wrestling with right now? End your psalm with exaltation because God is about to do something great!

DO I NEED A DAY OF REST?

BY PASTOR BRAD LIEBE

I AM THE LORD YOUR GOD; FOLLOW MY DECREES AND BE CAREFUL TO KEEP MY LAWS. KEEP MY SABBATHS HOLY, THAT THEY MAY BE A SIGN BETWEEN US. THEN YOU WILL KNOW THAT I AM THE LORD YOUR GOD.

EZEKIEL 20:19-20 (NIV)

Genesis Chapter 1 tells us how God created the heavens and earth. If there is a moment I would like to go back and see, outside of the resurrection of Jesus Christ, it would be when God created the world. Seeing God speak light into existence and call it good would be incredible. Could you imagine watching God bring the land up from the water, creating dry ground? How amazing would it be to see the species of animals, fish, birds, trees, flowers, bushes, and grass emerge from nothing and populate the earth?

Yet on day seven, God does something unusual, He rests. He worked for six days and then rested on the seventh. Isaiah 40 tells us that God never grows weak or weary, so the purpose of the Sabbath was not for Him but for us. Jesus affirmed that when He came to earth.

On one Sabbath, Jesus and His disciples walked through a grain field. His disciples were picking off heads of grain and eating them, which caused the Pharisees to scoff because they called it "harvesting," a form of work. The Pharisees had misconceptions about the work that could be done on the Sabbath. For instance, some believed taking too many steps on the Sabbath would be considered work.

Jesus said, "The Sabbath was made for man, not man for the Sabbath." Jesus told the Pharisees that God did not make the Sabbath and declared, "I need someone to keep this day holy; I'll make humans!" Instead, God created the Sabbath for our benefit, to help us.

How should a Sabbath day be structured? It is a day of rest but not laziness. On our Sabbath day, we should worship the Lord, read and meditate on His words, practice communion by remembering Christ's death and resurrection, ask God to speak to us, and spend time praying. We should practice solitude and silence on the Sabbath to hear His voice.

Nothing is wrong with doing good or serving others on the Sabbath; it should be an extension of our worship. However, our Sabbath should be focused on God. He wants you to rest so you can recharge to do what He wants. He desires to speak to you and wants you to take the time to listen.

→ MOVING FORWARD

Schedule a day for your Sabbath and create a plan for the day. Stay focused on God; your Sabbath will be refreshing, invigorating, and eye-opening.

IT'S A PROCESS

BY PASTOR DANIEL GARRISON

MY EYES ARE EVER ON THE LORD, FOR ONLY HE WILL RELEASE MY FEET FROM THE SNARE.

PSALM 25:15 (NIV)

When meditating on God's Word, my mind interprets that as "work the Scripture repeatedly in your mind...and ask lots of questions." With that in mind, walk with me through a metaphor.

Imagine yourself in a forest in the springtime. The weather is excellent, flowers are in bloom, and birds are chirping in the trees—what a day to be outdoors. While walking, you step on a bear trap! Oh no, your leg is caught! You try your hardest to free yourself from the trap but can't. You cry out for help! Enter Jesus. He comes over, pulls the trap open, and releases your leg.

Pause While this sums up what we find in this verse, meditating on it reveals more truth, wisdom, and encouragement. *Unpause*

Now, once you're freed from this trap, you're undoubtedly incapable of running or walking; you've got a wound that must be addressed. It must be cleaned, set straight, and mended. This process takes time; if not treated, it may get infected, or you may be left with a limp. So take care. After this process, your leg is restored, and you can walk and run again. All that's left is a scar, a reminder of what previously trapped you. But praise be to God, the One who hears our cries and not only releases us from the enemy's snares but restores us to health.

How does this apply to us? I'm so glad you asked. We are all somewhere in this process. We are trapped in something or need to be freed. We need to be healed or freshly healed on the other side of recovery.

So, where do you find yourself?

Trapped? – God can bring freedom.

Need healing? – God can restore and mend the broken.

Were you left with a scar? – That's your testimony! The story of where you used to be. "Look! Look at what craziness I was once in! And let me tell you how my God set me free."

Wherever you find yourself in the process of healing and restoration, reach out to God and ask Him to be part of the process. He can do more than bring freedom. God promises to heal you and give you a powerful testimony to help people see Him.

→ MOVING FORWARD

Ask God to be a part of your healing process. Write it down and share it with a close friend, allowing them to join your journey. They'll experience your testimony, and you'll experience His freedom!

GREAT POWER AND GREAT GRACE

BY PASTOR DAWSON OQUIST

WITH GREAT POWER THE APOSTLES CONTINUED TO TESTIFY TO THE RESURRECTION OF THE LORD JESUS. AND GOD'S GRACE WAS SO POWERFULLY AT WORK IN THEM ALL.

ACTS 4:33 (NIV)

The word *power* can carry a negative connotation with it. We think of quotes like:

"Power concedes nothing without a demand."

"Power is always dangerous. It attracts the worst and corrupts the best."

And "Power tends to corrupt, and absolute power corrupts absolutely."

History is full of people using power for injustice, selfish gains, and unspeakable atrocities. But we see in the Book of Acts a new kind of power: not one that takes away freedom but offers it to those whom it contacts. This power wasn't used to force, disenfranchise, or dominate anyone. Instead, this life-giving power was used to show the world the truth that Jesus is alive.

This same power was present in Jesus throughout His life on earth. It is the same power that raised Him from the dead, the same power that was poured out in Acts 2 on the day of Pentecost, and the same power that you and I are given when we say yes to Jesus and receive the Holy Spirit. But it isn't that power alone that changes the world. The key is God's grace.

You see, the people of that day knew what power looked like; they lived under the rule and reign of the mighty Roman Empire. But to witness a more significant power administered with—not coercion, but grace—was what allowed a ragtag band of fishermen to change the world from the ground up. And it's what can change the world again.

→ MOVING FORWARD

This week, make it your prayer for God to endow you with a new sense of both His power and His grace. Step out with boldness. Be gracious to all. Accept that God wants to advance His Kingdom through you.

TAKE THE INITIATIVE TO DRAW NEAR TO GOD

BY PASTOR MORENA CASTRO

**BUT AS FOR ME, IT IS GOOD TO BE NEAR GOD.
I HAVE MADE THE SOVEREIGN LORD MY REFUGE;
I WILL TELL OF ALL YOUR DEEDS.**

PSALM 73:28 (NIV)

When you think of the Book of Psalms, what comes to mind? Perhaps you think of peaceful pastures, fiery turmoil, exuberant thanksgiving, or anguished complaints? All of these apply to this collection of poems given to us by God to help narrate our life experiences. When we read the Psalms, it is essential to remember why they were written. They reflect real feelings expressed to a real God about real life.

In Psalm 73, Asaph was struggling with the idea of wicked people being successful in this life. He was going through these moments because he believed God was good, but when Asaph looked around, he saw the righteous suffer, and the wicked prosper. Have you ever had a similar experience?

When God's character seems to be at odds with the circumstances around us, we must seek God for His perspective and have an unshakable conviction of God's goodness. When we take the initiative to worship God and seek His face, He sustains us.

The psalmist introduces God as someone near to us. Even when we are going through something challenging and our emotions declare the opposite, He is close to us. Our adoration must continue to be active, seeking His presence and remaining in His love. A life away from God will not produce anything in a person.

Relying entirely on God's power is a sign of intimacy. We will grow closer when we share our feelings, put our trust in Him, and believe. Approaching God gives us security even when we find ourselves in stormy days. Intimacy comes with trust and results in more faith and works.

Are you tapping into the Biblical resource of the Psalms as the incredible tool it is to establish an intimate relationship with God? In the midst of whatever you're facing, take the initiative to seek God with all your heart, long for His presence, and find it in prayer. He will respond with love, intimacy, and peace.

→ MOVING FORWARD

Ask God to lead you to a Psalm today. As you read its words, make them your own. Pray the words of Scripture back to God, asking Him to speak to you as you take refuge in Him.

WHO DO YOU IMITATE?

BY JONI OQUIST

IMITATE GOD, THEREFORE, IN EVERYTHING YOU DO, BECAUSE YOU ARE HIS DEAR CHILDREN. LIVE A LIFE FILLED WITH LOVE, FOLLOWING THE EXAMPLE OF CHRIST. HE LOVED US AND OFFERED HIMSELF AS A SACRIFICE FOR US, A PLEASING AROMA TO GOD.

EPHESIANS 5:1-2 (NLT)

Soon after my parents became "empty-nesters," my father picked up a new hobby by becoming the proud owner of a cockatiel named "Pokey." Dad enjoyed spending time caring for his bird and endeavored to teach his talking pet words, phrases, and songs. It was amazing how Pokey would imitate Mom and Dad, sometimes quite humorously.

One evening, as my parents were hosting a small group in their home, Dad told the story of Creation. At a pivotal point in the message, he asked, "How do you think Adam responded when he first saw Eve?" On cue, Pokey broke into one of his favorite songs, *"Hey, good lookin', whatcha got cookin'?"* The Bible study was cut short as the group could not stop laughing!

Like my dad's bird, I too have a habit of imitating the words and phrases of those I spend significant time with. My daughter has my mannerisms, and my son sounds like his dad when he preaches. In today's reading, the Apostle Paul takes this topic to a whole other level by encouraging his friends in Ephesus to imitate God by following the example of Christ.

Imitate means "to follow as a pattern, model, or example," but how is it possible to imitate Christ? Practically speaking, we learn to imitate Jesus as we study His life and then practice doing what He did. Spiritually speaking, we depend on Him through prayer and are empowered by the Holy Spirit.

Whenever we see the word "therefore" in a verse, it's a cue to reflect on the previous verses. In chapter four of Ephesians, Paul encourages his readers to live lives worthy of the calling they've received from Christ. While He walked this earth, Jesus showed us how to imitate God through how He lived and loved. Ephesians 4:32 tells us to be kind and compassionate to one another and to forgive each other just as Christ has forgiven us. Kindness, compassion, and forgiveness are just a few of Christ's many attributes. Above all, He desires us to follow His example by living a life of love and sacrifice.

Who do *you* imitate? Can others tell that you are a follower of Jesus? If you've picked up some bad habits along the way or are involved in behavior that doesn't display the nature of Christ, I encourage you to take a moment for some reflection.

→ MOVING FORWARD

Take an honest assessment. If your attitudes and actions don't match your Savior's, apologize and ask for His help. God wants to help you become more like Christ Jesus.

GOD'S PERFECT TIMING

BY PASTOR TERRY TOWNSEND

YOU SEE, AT JUST THE RIGHT TIME, WHEN WE WERE STILL POWERLESS, CHRIST DIED FOR THE UNGODLY.

ROMANS 5:6 (NIV)

Lawrence Punter, a friend of mine, was a star. But he was a star with secrets. Lawrence was born to parents who didn't want him. When he was three months old, they shipped him off to live with his grandmother on the island of Antigua.

He had a happy childhood there until, at seven years old, he was sent back to New York City to live with his mother. Because he reminded her of the unfaithful husband who abandoned her, she physically and verbally abused him. At school, he was highly timid because he spoke with a West Indian accent. He felt all alone in the world and was bullied mercilessly. In middle school, he was forced to join a gang, where he surprisingly found the "family" he longed for. Now everyone at school was afraid of him! But there was a dark side. One night there was an all-out battle, and the opposing gang severely beat him. Fearing he would die or be imprisoned, his mother took him to Miami, where he blossomed, becoming a basketball MVP and an All-American with scholarship offers.

But things would take another turn. In Lawrence's sophomore year of college, he suffered a leg injury and lost his scholarship. Lawrence moved to Tulsa, where he washed dishes at Denny's while attending flight school. But he lost his job, had to move out of his apartment, and couldn't pay for school. When he ran out of friends' couches to crash on, he lived in an alley next to his old apartment, sleeping on a mattress he found by a dumpster. His only income was selling plasma at the blood bank for seven dollars. He was now surviving on loaves of bread.

He began to replay the words of his mother: "You're no good, nothing but a big zero, just like your father."

All her predictions had come true, and sleep was his only escape. This time when he sold his plasma, he purchased a bottle of sleeping pills, intending to make his pain go away forever. He sat on the mattress with the pills in one hand and a bottle of water in the other. Then, he heard the sound of a TV in an apartment above him, from which he heard a man's voice saying, "God loves you. Jesus Christ gave his life for you." The words reached him in his pain, and he let Jesus into his life. He felt a peace he never knew.

God met him in a powerful way and changed his life at just the right moment.

→ MOVING FORWARD

What was your rock bottom moment? How did God meet you there? Are you at the bottom today? Consider and take heart: When you praise God at the bottom, it's not the bottom anymore!

GIVING GOD OUR GRIEF

BY PASTOR JASON BRIESACHER

THE LORD IS CLOSE TO THE BROKENHEARTED;
HE RESCUES THOSE WHOSE SPIRITS ARE CRUSHED.

PSALM 34:18 (NLT)

My grandpa had a significant impact on my life. He was a wise counselor and loving friend who led me to Jesus and helped me become a better father, husband, and man. He passed in December 2021. The loss was devastating.

The moment he passed, I celebrated. After two decades of battling severe illnesses, he crossed the threshold into heaven. What a joyous victory! Then I realized I would have to live without him for the rest of my life. Grief set in and still sweeps over me as I write this devotional.

Grief is an emotional anomaly. There is no other emotion quite like it. When you confront fear, it goes away. Sadness can be modified by a good day or a kind word. Anger and happiness come and go; you never feel the same way you did when those feelings arose. But grief holds strong like an anchor. Its grip brings us back to the moment of loss and envelops our moods and senses. A great day is overshadowed by mourning, and the happiest moments still have a tinge of sorrow attached to them.

Reflect for a moment on two instances in Jesus' life when He expressed grief. One was when He looked at Jerusalem and said He wanted to draw the people to Himself like a hen gathers her chicks. Jesus lamented the relationship lost between humanity and God. The second time was when Jesus learned His friend Lazarus had died. I always thought it odd that Jesus, who already declared He would raise Lazarus, broke down sobbing when approaching the tomb. I used to think it was because others were grieving, but I believe it was due to death itself. God didn't design our bodies to die; I think Jesus was lamenting humanity's fate because of sin.

Jesus came to remedy both of those situations. He came to obliterate death's sting and to remove the barrier between God and man. Yet, in the midst of this, the grief remained. Hebrews tells us that we have Jesus Christ, our High Priest, who understands our struggles. He understands your suffering.

Grief isn't only experienced over the loss of a person; it can happen whenever there is a loss of any kind: a job, a relationship, or an unexpected diagnosis. Letting Him into your grief is the only way toward healing. He understands and wants to help. Don't hold on to it alone, struggling in silence; let the Wonderful Counselor do His work.

→ MOVING FORWARD

Tell God about your grief; give Him all your emotions. When they come up again, talk to Him again. His presence won't change the loss, but He'll envelop you in His love.

GET IN THE RIVER

BY PASTOR MATT MARKARIAN

BE STRONG AND COURAGEOUS, BECAUSE YOU WILL LEAD THESE PEOPLE TO INHERIT THE LAND I SWORE TO THEIR ANCESTORS TO GIVE THEM.

JOSHUA 1:6 (NIV)

In the Book of Joshua, we see the Israelites standing at the edge of the Promised Land, ready to enter and conquer it. This land was promised to Abraham, Isaac, and Jacob. The Israelites had been waiting for this moment for more than 400 years. However, their leader, Moses, had died, and now Joshua was tasked with leading the Israelites into the Promised Land.

As Joshua stood on the edge of the Jordan River, God spoke to him, saying, "Moses, my servant, is dead. Now then, you and all these people, get ready to cross the Jordan River into the land I am about to give to them—to the Israelites" (Joshua 1:2). God then gave Joshua a message of encouragement and instruction, telling him to be strong and courageous and to lead the people in obedience to God's commands.

This passage repeats the command to be strong and courageous three times, highlighting its importance. God knew that Joshua would face many challenges, obstacles, and insecurities as he led the Israelites into the Promised Land. Therefore, God encouraged Joshua to be strong and courageous, reminding him that God would be with him wherever he went.

The strength and courage to which God called Joshua were not simply physical attributes. Instead, they were qualities of the heart and soul. To be strong and courageous, Joshua would need to trust in God's promises, meditate on God's Word, and obey God's commands.

Just as Joshua faced challenges and obstacles, we too, will face difficult life situations. It may be health crises, financial troubles, relationship problems, or other difficulties. However, God's message to Joshua is still relevant to us today. We too must be strong and courageous, trusting in God's promises, meditating on God's Word, and obeying God's commands.

In times of trouble, it is easy to become discouraged or afraid. However, we can find strength and courage in God's promises. We can trust that God is with us, just as He was with Joshua. We can meditate on God's Word, allowing it to strengthen and encourage us. And we can obey God's commands, knowing that obedience leads to blessings and success.

→ MOVING FORWARD

As we face life's challenges, remember God's command to be strong and courageous. Trust God's promises, meditate on His Word, and obey His commands.

TAKE A DEEP BREATH

BY PASTOR DJ OQUIST

HE SAYS, "BE STILL, AND KNOW THAT I AM GOD."

PSALM 46:10A (NIV)

Have you ever experienced a moment of utter stillness? Perhaps it was while you were alone, out in the sanctuary of nature. All of a sudden, everything seems to drop away, and you find yourself in an atmosphere of total serenity. Silence can be powerful; the inner calm and quietude of a heart stilled by the presence of Almighty God are much more so.

I love to get things done. At the end of a long day, I can go home feeling good if I have accomplished all the items on my to-do list. Whether or not you relate to this, I believe we all want to feel there's forward movement in our lives—that we are making a difference each day. And nothing is wrong with feeling accomplished! It only becomes a problem if it competes with what our greatest priority should be: spending time with God.

This verse is God responding to the psalmist as he faces an overwhelming circumstance revealed in the previous verses. "God is our refuge and strength, an ever-present help in trouble; therefore, we will not fear." As he continues to write, you can sense the emotions he has been feeling about his next challenge. In response, God says, "Be still, and know that I am God."

I wonder how many of us simply miss what God is doing because we are moving too fast to perceive it. Amid everything going on in our lives, we know the most important thing is God. Yet how often do we miss what *He* is doing because we are too focused on what *we* are doing? The first time we ever came to God, it was that we might surrender our lives to Him. So why can't we take a moment to submit our most significant obstacles to Him as well?

This only happens as we intentionally pause to focus on Him.

→ MOVING FORWARD

Ask God to reveal things in your life that distract you from Him, and adjust how you spend your time. Then, take a deep breath. Whatever you are facing, pause, and surrender it to God.

BETWEEN THE GENERATIONS

BY PASTOR DALE OQUIST

THE HUMAN BODY HAS MANY PARTS, BUT THE MANY PARTS MAKE UP ONE WHOLE BODY. SO IT IS WITH THE BODY OF CHRIST.

1 CORINTHIANS 12:12 (NLT)

One of the things I love most about Peoples Church is that we are intentionally multigenerational. There is power in bringing together generations to live life together and engage with one another. Young people want to share their knowledge and experience with the older generation. More seasoned individuals crave the bond of being a wise counselor to a younger leader.

The Bible commands us to share God's goodness, might, wonders, deeds, and laws repeatedly. It tells us to share it from generation to generation. This knowledge was shared organically hundreds of years ago because education came from the home; there was no corporate school structure. Think of how much easier that would have been for parents and elders if they were already spending time with children, teaching them to become carpenters or blacksmiths.

As we have modernized the education process, we find ourselves more segregated. Kids go to school, parents work, and the family gets together when possible. We do this at church as well! We have programs for kids, students, college age, young adults, married couples, singles, and people with special needs. These programs create opportunities for each group to learn in an environment that suits them, where they can hear the gospel in a language and level appropriate for them.

Knowing that we are more segregated, we must act intentionally to connect generations. This relationship isn't the responsibility of Peoples Church as an organization; this is the responsibility of the people who make up Peoples Church. *It is up to you!*

Young people: Don't wait for a mentor to appear; introduce yourself to someone older than you. Elders: Don't wait for an invitation to join a ministry! Build a relationship with someone younger than you and take them to lunch; that's a unique ministry! We are one body working together; it's time to share that unity.

Both young and old should share what God has done in their lives and point one another toward Jesus. Take the time to listen to each other and learn something new. This purposeful exchange will unite generations and create something special at Peoples Church. We will find more understanding, conversation, and growth when we share what God has done among the generations.

→ MOVING FORWARD

Find someone younger and older, ask them to have coffee or a meal, and share your testimony with them, which is a powerful reminder of God's faithfulness. It helps us push forward when we invite others on our journey.

TRUST THE PROCESS

BY PASTOR MATT PERKINS

FOR I AM ABOUT TO DO SOMETHING NEW. SEE, I HAVE ALREADY BEGUN! DO YOU NOT SEE IT? I WILL MAKE A PATHWAY THROUGH THE WILDERNESS. I WILL CREATE RIVERS IN THE DRY WASTELAND.

ISAIAH 43:19 (NLT)

Let's face it: change is difficult. Even in the best circumstances, change can leave us feeling like everything is shifting and unfamiliar. We can even pray for a particular change to happen in our life, and then when it presents itself, we instinctively try to hold on tight to what is routine and comfortable, even if it may not be the best for us.

When we face transitions and change in life, here are a few things to keep in mind:

Preparation
God is about to do something new. It is up to us to prepare for what God has arranged for us. Hint: He plans to prosper you and not harm you (Jeremiah 29:11).

Perception
We must be aware and attentive as God brings "the new" into our lives. If you aren't looking for it, you could easily miss what God desires to do because it's so natural for us to focus on the status quo.

Provision
Whenever God brings new vision and direction, He will also provide a way. This Scripture clearly states that God will make a way where there doesn't seem to be one.

Patience

We need to trust the process. Trusting the process can be difficult, but as we walk by faith, knowing that we're on the path of God's choosing, we will get closer to our destination day by day.

As I reflect on this passage of Scripture, I am reminded of the first verse of "'Tis So Sweet to Trust in Jesus."

'Tis so sweet to trust in Jesus
Just to take Him at His Word
Just to rest upon His promise
Just to know, thus saith the Lord

Getting through uncertain moments with peace, wisdom, and appreciation for all that lies ahead is necessary and only possible through His grace.

→ MOVING FORWARD

Ask God where your trust level is. What areas of your life can you more intentionally place in His care? Sing the words of this beloved hymn, and ask for grace to trust Him more.

MAKING ROOM

BY PASTOR BRAD LIEBE

UNLESS THE LORD BUILDS A HOUSE, THE WORK OF THE BUILDERS IS WASTED. UNLESS THE LORD PROTECTS A CITY, GUARDING IT WITH SENTRIES WILL DO NO GOOD. IT IS USELESS FOR YOU TO WORK SO HARD FROM EARLY MORNING UNTIL LATE AT NIGHT, ANXIOUSLY WORKING FOR FOOD TO EAT; FOR GOD GIVES REST TO HIS LOVED ONES.

PSALM 127:1-2 (NLT)

I am a workaholic. I'm in the process of recovery, but I'm overcoming decades of habits and tendencies. I looked at 2 Thessalonians 3, where Paul repeats the adage, "If a man does not work, he should not eat," and I ran with it. This philosophy spoke to me as a Midwestern American Christian! I thought, "If it is godly to work and I work more, then I'll become godlier!"

It's not true. The longer I work, the less I become like Jesus Christ.

As Christians, we should be hard workers. Paul reminds us in Colossians that we are representatives of Jesus Christ and should work as if we are working for Him. As we work, there will be seasons when you work harder than others; for instance, farmers work harder during the harvest than in the winter.

As Americans living in 2023, we have filled our days with work, activities, and entertainment. There isn't a lot of time that we sit quietly throughout our day, and it's starting to harm our spirit. We are inundated with noise and have lost the ability to hear God's voice. We're overworked and overstimulated. The good news is, we can fix it!

As you start your day, connect with God. Read a devotional and your Bible, pray, and listen for His voice. As you drive from place to place, turn off your podcast or music and talk with God in a two-way conversation. Ask Him questions and listen to His responses.

Before you pray, send that email, answer that call, submit that assignment, or do anything, check in with your Heavenly Father. God's trying to speak to you and wants to help you throughout the day. We will find His guidance when we learn to listen to His voice.

We cannot work and toil without asking the Master what He wants. Some days, He'll tell you to work hard and work long hours. On other days, He'll ask you to go home and connect with your kids. Still, at other times, He'll tell you what to say at work to impact the people around you.

Jesus told us that if we placed God as our number one priority throughout the day, He would give us everything we needed. He will help us set our priorities and move through our day with His presence, strength, and wisdom.

➡ MOVING FORWARD

Ask God for His guidance for today. Ask Him what He wants you to do at work, school, home, or on the road. Make room for His Spirit to work on you and help you become more like Christ Jesus.

COME TO ME

BY PASTOR MORENA CASTRO

COME TO ME, ALL YOU WHO ARE WEARY AND BURDENED, AND I WILL GIVE YOU REST. TAKE MY YOKE UPON YOU AND LEARN FROM ME, FOR I AM GENTLE AND HUMBLE IN HEART, AND YOU WILL FIND REST FOR YOUR SOULS. FOR MY YOKE IS EASY AND MY BURDEN IS LIGHT.

MATTHEW 11:28-30 (NIV)

Pressure. It's a word that brings to mind uncomfortable scenarios, such as extreme temperatures and cumbersome burdens. Regardless of our profession or ministry, challenges will always be present in the life of a Christian. Each of us is subjected to pressure according to our capacity. Amid it all, we are called to live from glory to glory. Yet, we can easily get caught up in activities, burdening ourselves.

Prioritizing problems instead of God inevitably places us under a heavy burden. The weight of this burden is the equivalent of putting the cart before the horse! Trying to do it all alone, we carry these burdens in our own strength. However, when we spend time with God, He'll ask us to give up these burdens and carry His load, which is light. This surrender only happens when we are in the right relationship with Him.

Because of His loving-kindness, nothing is more important than our fellowship with God. We sometimes prioritize our families, jobs, ministries, or activities over our relationship with God. But He designed us to live in connection with Him. It would be as ridiculous as having a friend you couldn't hug or a bicycle you couldn't ride. God gave us this relationship with Him to enjoy it!

God, Jesus, and the Holy Spirit are the source of our lives. The Father gives authority and anointing; the Son gives love and rest. The Holy

Spirit gives power and revelation. Only in this relationship do we find the tools to carry out what has been entrusted to us.

Have you felt overwhelmed lately—as if there are only burdens in your life? That means you are carrying your yoke instead of allowing Jesus to shoulder it. What is the solution? *Come to Him.* Give Him everything, and ask Him to give you His yoke in exchange. This yoke never weighs you down. It is so light that it's a joy to carry, not a burden.

Are you finding this difficult to do? Remember this always: the day of your salvation. The day you realized Jesus is all you needed to be fulfilled.

→ MOVING FORWARD

When was the last time you talked with God and waited to hear His response? Search for Him with all your heart. Step away from your planned activity today and return to the path of His Spirit.

GOD DOESN'T NEED YOU

BY PASTOR JÄN VAN OOSTEN

THE GOD WHO MADE THE WORLD AND EVERYTHING IN IT IS THE LORD OF HEAVEN AND EARTH AND DOES NOT LIVE IN TEMPLES BUILT BY HUMAN HANDS. AND HE IS NOT SERVED BY HUMAN HANDS, AS IF HE NEEDED ANYTHING. RATHER, HE HIMSELF GIVES EVERYONE LIFE AND BREATH AND EVERYTHING ELSE.

ACTS 17:24-25 (NIV)

Let's face it; most Christians want to know that God cares about our challenges. The Bible says that Jesus can "empathize with our weaknesses" (Hebrews 4:15). When He was on earth, Jesus went through all kinds of difficulties, so He "gets it." However, we need to be careful not to think of God as a bigger, faster, smarter one of us. God is not a Marvel superhero like Thor.

Theologians have an odd word to describe something amazing about God: "aseity." Webster's Dictionary defines "aseity" as God's "absolute self-sufficiency, independence, and autonomy." In short, this means God is not dependent on anything or anybody. He is entirely self-sufficient and has absolutely no needs at all. In contrast, we have lots of needs. We need food, shelter, warmth, and, of course, we need love. God has no requirements, and we cannot do anything for Him that He cannot do Himself.

His autonomy raises the question: Why did God create us if He doesn't need us? Are you ready for the answer? Here it is: God created the universe, and all of us, out of His abundant, overflowing love. Great Christian thinkers like Augustine and Aquinas pointed out that our existence is a powerful message of God's love. The fact that you are alive right now means that God loves you. He brought you into existence.

So, yes, God doesn't need you. It is silly to think He does. Yet, your existence is a loud message telling you that God loves and cares about you. And beyond that, the only begotten Son of God, Jesus Christ, sympathizes with you through tough times.

→ MOVING FORWARD

Begin today to see yourself as truly loved by God. Don't let life's challenges and difficulties get you down. Know that God's love comes to us expressed through Jesus, who truly "gets it" and can help you. Turn to Him for help and guidance.

WHO IS BEAUTIFUL?

BY PASTOR CAMELIA CROSS

GUARD YOUR HEART ABOVE ALL ELSE, FOR IT DETERMINES THE COURSE OF YOUR LIFE.

PROVERBS 4:23 (NLT)

The Hebrew word "levav" is the most common word for "heart." It includes our thoughts, wills, discernment, and affections. Fascinating. Pondering this Scripture, "Guard your heart above all else", we ask ourselves, "Is this a suggestion?" Easy answer: *No, it's a command.* Who gave this command? *God did.* Who is responsible for doing the guarding? *Each of us.*

How important is this command? It says "above all." OK, that's self-explanatory. And based on the Hebrew meaning of the word "heart," we are to guard our thoughts, wills, discernment, and affections.

In this world, we need the help and guidance of the Holy Spirit to guard our hearts successfully! And we need the truth of God's Word to be the screen through which perceptions, thoughts, acts of will, and affections are evaluated. This world plays for keeps, and the enemy of our souls has a diabolical goal: to discourage and destroy us through thoughts. But as each idea comes to us, we can guard our hearts and ask, "Based on what the Bible says about who we are in Jesus, how much God loves us, and the good He has planned for us, is this a thought to keep or throw out as trash?"

And we can ask ourselves, "Is this affection bringing me closer to Jesus? Would what I'm about to do or say honor the Lord and encourage others to know Jesus because they see something different about how I handle the hard stuff of life?" As we guard our hearts, we must ask, "Did that thought sound like my loving Father or

Lord Jesus? Or was it trash?" The Holy Spirit will help us think about what we are thinking about!

What we focus on, we will become. Who is the most beautiful? Who has the most beautiful heart? We know, don't we? It's Jesus. Just look at how He loved and cared for the weak, hurting, and outcasts and gave them grace. He was gentle, yet firm and steady, moving with purpose to do His Father's will. He guarded His heart, and His heart is beautiful.

We must live the same way, and with the Holy Spirit's guidance in guarding our hearts, we can become more like Jesus. His leadership will make the difference in how we think and who we are.

→ MOVING FORWARD

Philippians 4:6-8 tells us what to think about. Read this and see if your thought-life measures up. Watch for the word "heart" throughout Scripture, and study the teachings involved. *It's fascinating!*

LIVING LIFE, SOWING SEEDS

BY PASTOR TERRY TOWNSEND

BUT HOW CAN THEY CALL ON HIM TO SAVE THEM UNLESS THEY BELIEVE IN HIM? AND HOW CAN THEY BELIEVE IN HIM IF THEY HAVE NEVER HEARD ABOUT HIM? AND HOW CAN THEY HEAR ABOUT HIM UNLESS SOMEONE TELLS THEM?

ROMANS 10:14 (NLT)

Reading Romans 10:14, we see Paul asking three rhetorical questions with three apparent answers.

THEY CAN'T:

- Call on God to save them if they don't believe in Him.
- Believe in Him until they hear about Him.
- Hear about Him until another person tells them about Him.

Back in the 1980s, when I was a student ministries pastor, this verse began to make sense to me. I realized that way too much of my time was spent with people who believed like me. These people were my tribe. We spoke the same language. It was *comfortable* for me. But all of a sudden, 'comfortable' wasn't good enough. My comfort had to change if I was going to make a difference. I saw the need to become *un*comfortable with my life, uncomfortable enough to put a world map on my wall and start praying for the entire world.

I can't tell you exactly how it happened, but within three years, our family was on the way to Indonesia, the largest Muslim country in the world. And I knew God was leading us there!

Fast-forward 30 years: I had just turned 60. Lila and I were speaking at a convention and arranged to have lunch with a friend Lila had grown up with. She lived in a beautiful high-rise, riverfront building with amazing views. It seemed like she had it all!

As we talked, the conversation lagged, and it became apparent that she was blind to the beauty around her. She just seemed empty. After finishing lunch, we drove away with Lila grieving over the friend she now barely recognized.

I was agitated as I turned to Lila and said, "We've got to live our lives purposefully! I will write a personal vision statement for the rest of my life." It was the wake-up call I needed.

Over the next few days, I struggled to put my thoughts into words, finally writing, "Because the Gospel is for everyone, I will live to take it to those who don't have access to it." Since that day, these words have encouraged me, sometimes corrected me, and constantly challenged me to improve. Even as I write this, I realize how short I've fallen.

→ MOVING FORWARD

Have you created a personal vision statement? If not, I challenge you to write your own. If you're anything like me, it will help to keep you on track.

HOW YOU HANDLE PRESSURE DEFINES YOUR FAITH

BY PASTOR LARRY POWELL

CONSIDER IT PURE JOY, MY BROTHERS AND SISTERS, WHENEVER YOU FACE TRIALS OF MANY KINDS, BECAUSE YOU KNOW THAT THE TESTING OF YOUR FAITH PRODUCES PERSEVERANCE. LET PERSEVERANCE FINISH ITS WORK SO THAT YOU MAY BE MATURE AND COMPLETE, NOT LACKING ANYTHING.

JAMES 1:2-4 (NIV)

It was June of 1949. An exploding epidemic of polio swept through the United States. One of the highest-profiled individuals on earth, President Franklin Delano Roosevelt, contracted polio and made treating it a high priority. I was 15 months old and had been walking since I was six months old. But one day that June, I could walk; the next day, I could not. Polio had struck again.

I can only imagine the pressure my parents must have felt. Their firstborn son had contracted polio, and their second unborn son had possibly been exposed to the danger. But they trusted the Lord amid their trial. What a remarkable example!

We are not to be caught up in the despair of pressures and negative circumstances, as those in the world so often are. On the surface, James does not make sense to most people: *Consider it pure joy when you face trials of many kinds.* Do you feel like jumping up and down with pure joy when things are not going well with you? Do you feel pure joy when you're sick, lose a loved one, watch the bills pile up, or your car won't start when you just have to be somewhere?

James focuses on practical action in our faith and encourages God's people to act as Jesus would no matter what. For James, faith is not an abstract proposition but a steadfast trust in God that endures trials. Our adversities are in God's hands—intended for our maturity and edification. Our testing is not passive but rather active participation with the Lord as He works perseverance into us. As we grow, we realize the magnitude of God's power and understand that Christian joy accompanies these tests. Joy in life's most trying circumstances is not typical, but something greater is at work. God is transforming us into who He needs us to be.

Are you starting to get it? When things get tough, God's plans for us remain good. His purposes will accomplish something through us, demonstrating that nothing can stand in His way. Now I understand and rejoice in having had polio. He was producing the ability to be who He wanted me to be. I count it all joy.

→ MOVING FORWARD

Thank Him for the trial you're facing today, and allow Him to work as you walk through it. Do the unthinkable and count it pure joy as He builds perseverance in you.

LEAN INTO PRAYER

BY PASTOR DANIEL GARRISON

SINCE THE FIRST DAY YOU BEGAN TO PRAY FOR UNDERSTANDING AND TO HUMBLE YOURSELF BEFORE YOUR GOD, YOUR REQUEST HAS BEEN HEARD IN HEAVEN. I HAVE COME IN ANSWER TO YOUR PRAYER. BUT FOR TWENTY-ONE DAYS, THE SPIRIT PRINCE OF THE KINGDOM OF PERSIA BLOCKED MY WAY. THEN MICHAEL, ONE OF THE ARCHANGELS, CAME TO HELP ME, AND I LEFT HIM THERE WITH THE SPIRIT PRINCE OF THE KINGDOM OF PERSIA. NOW I AM HERE TO EXPLAIN...

DANIEL 10:12B-14A (NLT)

Prayer is one of those spiritual practices with which we can have a love-hate relationship. We know we ought to pray, but when we don't see results or don't think we've heard from heaven, we can get discouraged. I've been there; you've been there; we've all been there. Sometimes we feel like prayer is a last-ditch effort, what we fall back on after we've tried everything in our power to handle it.

I'd like to encourage you that prayer is quite the opposite. It is one of the most powerful things you can do! And in this section of Scripture, we get a unique perspective on prayer directly from an angel of the Lord who came to the prophet Daniel.

We can assume that Daniel had been praying for at least twenty-one days. TWENTY-ONE DAYS he was seeking the Lord with no answer. This angel showed up and said that heaven heard him from the moment he started, and this angel was sent in response. So, our first encouragement is that heaven does hear our prayers!

We have no idea what spiritual roadblocks lie between our current circumstances and the result of what we're praying for. In Daniel's case, some serious spiritual warfare held the angel up enough to justify an archangel showing up as backup! Our second encouragement is that our prayers loose things into the heavens that we may not be aware of. Lean into 1 Thessalonians 5:17 when it encourages us to pray continually!

The final encouragement is this: What if victory was seven prayers away? What if that friend coming with you to church was fourteen prayers away? What if that family member's salvation was twenty-one prayers away? This perspective changes things! Covering something in prayer doesn't seem so laborious because you know the heavens are loosed on their behalf every time you pray. There might be a lot of spiritual roadblocks to clear before you see the fulfillment, but it's worth it. Your family is worth it. Your friends are worth it.

→ MOVING FORWARD

Lean into prayer. Journal your prayers to tally how often you're praying for something. You'll be surprised at the results!

REMAIN TRUE TO THE FAITH

BY PASTOR DAWSON OQUIST

THEN THEY RETURNED TO LYSTRA, ICONIUM AND ANTIOCH, STRENGTHENING THE DISCIPLES AND ENCOURAGING THEM TO REMAIN TRUE TO THE FAITH. "WE MUST GO THROUGH MANY HARDSHIPS TO ENTER THE KINGDOM OF GOD," THEY SAID.

ACTS 14:21B-22 (NIV)

Sharing our faith is nerve-wracking—especially now when popular culture seems to be so decidedly against the Christian faith. It seems easier to hide our beliefs to avoid difficult conversations with family, co-workers, or neighbors. Paul also understands the difficulties of living out his beliefs, so he tells his followers, "We must go through many hardships to enter the kingdom of God." Not because hardships are a requirement for entry but because that is the reality of being a citizen of heaven here on earth.

Paul had just been to Antioch, Iconium, and Lystra and had experienced tremendous pushback. In obedience to God and their mission to preach the gospel, he and Barnabas were chased out of Antioch and Iconium, only for Paul to be stoned and presumed dead in Lystra. In true Paul fashion, he returns to each of those cities, encouraging believers to consider difficulties as the reality of their dual citizenship.

What about us? Have we, like Paul, counted the cost of being a true follower of Christ? If so, we should not be surprised that the world is opposed to the message we carry. We will face pushback; we should expect it. But let us not allow a fear of resistance and struggle to get in the way of advancing God's Kingdom in our circles of influence.

Pushback from the world is not the same as pushback from God. You and I are called to partner with God in His redemptive story, so let us remain true to the faith and actively participate in that ever-unfolding plan.

→ MOVING FORWARD

Talk to God about fears you need to overcome. Is a need to be liked keeping you silent? Or a negative experience from sharing your faith that still hurts? Bring them to the feet of Jesus today.

GOD'S GOODNESS

BY PASTOR JASON BRIESACHER

GIVE THANKS TO THE LORD, FOR HE IS GOOD!
HIS FAITHFUL LOVE ENDURES FOREVER.

1 CHRONICLES 16:34 (NLT)

The word "good" is thrown around in our world. "How was the meal?" "Good." The inevitable "Be good!" as you drop your kids off at school. From a young age, I remember hearing that God is good and thought it was inadequate. Wouldn't "great" fit God more than "good"? God's greatness is on display everywhere. The earth, His footstool, declares His majesty. The universe, which fits in the span of His hand, sings His praises. He is great, and His authority has no end.

While His greatness describes His power, His goodness describes the quality of His character. It is both an adjective and a verb. His goodness represents His kindness and mercy, gentleness and purity, and the standard of righteousness that makes evil flee. The goodness of God describes who He is at His core.

As an adjective, the goodness of God is seen in His righteousness and evil's aversion to Him. No choice He makes could be evil or come with malice because He's good. His motives are merciful, and His reasoning is pure. The consequences or outcomes of His choices will invariably be for your benefit because. *HE IS GOOD!*

When things are going well, we can feel the goodness of God. We stand on the mountaintop, declaring God is good. He acted on our behalf and blessed us! When life is great, it's easy to proclaim the goodness of God.

But the goodness of God is found not only on mountaintops but also in valleys. The depth of His goodness is found in moments of struggle.

He is good when the job has been lost, or the relationship has ended. When the sickness worsens, and loneliness sets in, He is good. When everything seems wrong around us, He is still good.

The goodness of God, as a verb, is not found in sweeping declarations but in intimate moments with Him, born from difficult circumstances. His active goodness is His grace and peace, His kindness and love. His active goodness has redeemed you and sets you free. When we are at the point of feeling we have nothing else, we still have His presence because He is good.

→ MOVING FORWARD

Take a moment to allow His Spirit to wash over you. Whether on the mountaintop or in the valley, declare that the Lord is good and His faithful love endures forever.

THE FLIP SIDE OF YOUR SPIRITUAL LIFE

BY PASTOR DALE OQUIST

**INSTRUCT THE WISE, AND THEY WILL BE EVEN WISER.
TEACH THE RIGHTEOUS, AND THEY WILL LEARN EVEN MORE.**

PROVERBS 9:9 (NLT)

As our world has grown and technology has increased our ability to communicate knowledge, we have more information at our fingertips than at any point in recorded history. We can study the cosmos at the touch of a button. Experts from every profession line up to share their understanding, with their thoughts being recorded and shared worldwide.

While exploring the intricacies of plant and animal life is fascinating, and discoveries at the bottom of the ocean are incredible, I would venture to say that the subject you most need to study lives within your own body—right between your ears. Your brain is an incredibly complex organ that houses your mind, which makes up your personality.

Your preferences, characteristics, strengths, and weaknesses come from this personality, which is directly connected to your spiritual life. If you are an extrovert, nothing binds you to God more than going to church and connecting with other believers. Talking with people and sharing your faith comes naturally; evangelism and faith-in-action are your strengths, but you struggle with silence and times of reflection.

If you're an introvert, evangelism seems daunting. You would avoid the Great Commission at all costs if you could find a way around it. You don't struggle to connect with God privately, and your quiet time is fantastic, but participation in small groups or corporate worship can be difficult at first.

Your personality and preferences led you toward those spiritual strengths, and God uses them for His glory and purpose. However, the flip side of your spiritual life should not be ignored. It will seem uncomfortable, but that is how we grow. If you are extroverted, you need quiet times when God can speak to you. If you are introverted, you must share your faith with a stranger. This stretching will be a blessing to you and to them as you testify to the goodness of God.

If we aren't careful, we will become one-sided Christians who only focus on our strengths while allowing the enemy to take a foothold in our lives. Let God stretch you, grow you, and help you become your strongest by strengthening the flip side of your spiritual life.

→ MOVING FORWARD

Take a personality quiz and see what your tendencies may be. Do you agree with the assessment? Write down spiritual practices you enjoy and ones you avoid, then plan to practice one you avoid today.

NOT FINISHED YET

BY PASTOR MATT PERKINS

BROTHERS AND SISTERS, I DO NOT CONSIDER MYSELF YET TO HAVE TAKEN HOLD OF IT. BUT ONE THING I DO: FORGETTING WHAT IS BEHIND AND STRAINING TOWARD WHAT IS AHEAD, I PRESS ON TOWARD THE GOAL TO WIN THE PRIZE FOR WHICH GOD HAS CALLED ME HEAVENWARD IN CHRIST JESUS.

PHILIPPIANS 3:13-14 (NIV)

In our walk with God, we often reflect on the victories and miracles He has done in our lives. While it's essential to appreciate and celebrate the ways God has moved in the past, we mustn't become so fixated on our history that we miss out on what He wants to do in our lives today. The Apostle Paul exhorts us to keep moving forward toward our ultimate objective. Reflect on these life-directing words: "Brothers and sisters, I do not consider myself yet to have taken hold of it. But one thing I do: Forgetting what is behind and straining toward what is ahead, I press on toward the goal to win the prize for which God has called me heavenward in Christ Jesus."

Paul's words are a powerful reminder that our journey with God is not stagnant. It is a dynamic, ever-evolving relationship, and we must be willing to embrace the new things He has in store for us. We need to deliberately remain open to God's continuous work in our lives and the changes that come with it. Our human nature often leads us to cling to our past experiences, whether successes or failures. If we are honest with ourselves, stepping out into the unknown can be very intimidating. However, when we allow ourselves to be governed by our past, we limit our growth potential. We hinder our development in our walk with God.

God is always doing something new in our lives, and we must trust Him to guide us through each season. This newness requires us to let go of our preconceived notions about our journey and allow God to mold and shape us according to His will.

Remember that God is not finished with you yet. As long as you have breath, there is more to learn, experience, and discover about His love, grace, and purpose for our lives. We must press on and actively pursue the goals and dreams He has placed in our hearts, trusting He will be with us every step.

→ MOVING FORWARD

What past experiences have you been holding in your mind? What pain are you holding on to that God wants to remove? Take a moment to ask Him about the new experiences He is leading you toward.

BE STILL

BY PASTOR BRAD LIEBE

**BE STILL, AND KNOW THAT I AM GOD!
I WILL BE HONORED BY EVERY NATION. I WILL BE
HONORED THROUGHOUT THE WORLD.**

PSALM 46:10 (NLT)

I want you to take a moment with me and imagine a different life for yourself before the invention of electricity. When we lived in a dawn-to-dusk world, you might be riding on a horse across the empty countryside. Perhaps you would work on a farm in the field. Some of you would work in town around others. Regardless of your profession, silence would fall every night. There would be moments to collect your thoughts and listen to God. Finding those moments of silence today, is hard.

Now, don't get me wrong, I love our modern conveniences. If I had to choose to live in any time period, it would have to be after the invention of electricity and indoor plumbing. But these conveniences come at the cost of built-in peace and quiet. These days, even if you're a cattle rustler on the plains, you can watch videos on your phone all night. We can fill our days with endless entertainment.

This struggle doesn't make our modern conveniences or technology inherently bad; it just means we must seek peace on purpose. There was a moment in the life of Elijah when he ended up at the mountain of God. There was a fire, an earthquake, and a significant wind, but God was not in those moments. After the blazing, ground-shaking, and ear-splitting moments, there was God's still, small voice. Elijah walked away changed.

We want peace and quiet in our lives, but our actions don't match our desires. Jesus is the Prince over peace. He owns peace and doles it out as He sees fit. If we aren't careful, we will drown out His voice and lose the peace that comes with the quiet. Can you sit, like Elijah, and allow His voice to change you?

Our verse for today tells us to "be still, and know that I am God." It is in a chapter and passage that talks about Israel's battles. It ends by telling us that God will be exalted overall. He told Israel, "I don't need YOU to do anything except be still. I will take care of the rest."

We need our silence and solitude. If closing yourself in your closet doesn't work, go for a walk. Don't listen to anything, including worship music. Ask God, "What do you want to say to me?" You'll be amazed by His response in His still, small voice.

→ MOVING FORWARD

Don't wait for tomorrow; start today with 15 minutes of solitude. Sit in a room or take a walk and unplug. Ask God to speak, listen for His gentle voice, and let His peace envelop you.

THE ONE FOR YOU IS GREATER

BY PASTOR TYLER VILLINES

"DON'T BE AFRAID," THE PROPHET ANSWERED. "THOSE WHO ARE WITH US ARE MORE THAN THOSE WHO ARE WITH THEM."

2 KINGS 6:16 (NIV)

In this passage, Elisha's servant wakes up and steps outside, recognizing that the army of the king of Syria surrounds them. The servant, realizing that any hope of fleeing from this army is lost, runs to Elisha, fearful of their impending doom. Elisha responds to the servant gently yet boldly: "Do not be afraid. Those who are with us are more than those who are with them." At that moment, the servant's eyes were opened, revealing the Army of the Lord, full of horses and chariots of fire standing between the enemy and themselves. Elisha and the servant were untouched by the armies; God gave the entire army over to Elisha's hands.

Have you ever woken up, and before you even had the chance to get out of bed or have a cup of coffee, you are bombarded with bad news? Before you even have the strength to get through a typical day, you feel as though everything is against you. The burdens and problems of yesterday have carried over and teamed up with the burdens and difficulties of today, and you feel outnumbered?

Let me encourage you today. It may feel like you are surrounded, but the One who is for you is far greater than what stands against you. Think about this for a moment. The all-powerful, all-knowing King of Kings, the Maker of the heavens and Earth, is FOR YOU. He is on YOUR team! If the God of creation is for us, then who and what shall we fear? What stands in our way that is greater or more powerful than our God? Nothing. This encouragement is a reminder that, though attacks come in the newness of morning or the terror of night, God is telling you to fear not, for He is fighting on your behalf. He is your defender. He is making a way.

God also desires that we look up and see what He is doing around us. Sometimes we can get so caught up in the stress that life brings that we are distracted from the prayers He is answering, the ways He is moving, and the evidence that He is with us. The more we spend time in the presence of Jesus and fix our eyes on Him, the more His protection and provision in our lives are revealed.

→ MOVING FORWARD

Today, ask the Lord, "God, show me how you are moving in my life." When you do, you will see how evident His love and provision truly are. Take time and write down what God is revealing to you.

WHO IS JESUS?

BY PASTOR JÄN VAN OOSTEN

"BUT WHAT ABOUT YOU?" HE ASKED. "WHO DO YOU SAY I AM?" SIMON PETER ANSWERED, "YOU ARE THE MESSIAH, THE SON OF THE LIVING GOD."

MATTHEW 16:15-16 (NIV)

I am sure you know that most people say they "like" Jesus. And many of them will say, "Jesus is great. I just don't like 'organized religion.'" You've probably noticed that many like to conjure up their own versions of Jesus. Some say He was a great teacher, a wonderful example, or a "rebel" against the power structures of His day. There are lots and lots of versions of Jesus. There is a tendency for all of us to make Jesus into something we are very comfortable with. However, the question is: *Who is this Jesus?*

One day, Jesus took His disciples to the coast and asked them to tell Him what the crowds were saying about Him. The disciples identified several crowdsourced versions of Jesus. But then Jesus popped the tough question that all of us must answer, "Who do you say I am?" Our answer to that simple question is what separates all of humanity into one of two groups. The division is between those who "create their own Jesus" and those who submit to the true Jesus.

Peter got it right. Jesus is the Messiah, the Son of the Living God, who has come into the world to save sinners and be the Lord of their lives. Have you gotten it right? The easy thing is to make up our version of Jesus and go on "doing life." However, when we stop and realize who Jesus is, as described in the Bible, it demands a heartfelt response. The real Jesus came to save sinners, which all of us are. To have a genuine relationship with Jesus, I must admit that I am a sinner and submit to His leadership.

→ MOVING FORWARD

The Bible says that "every knee will bow and tongue confess" Jesus is Lord (Philippians 2:10-11). Have you? Kneel before Him to admit and submit if you haven't. Then share the good news of Jesus with others.

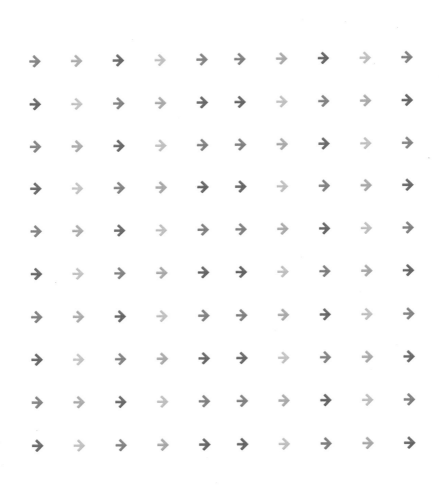